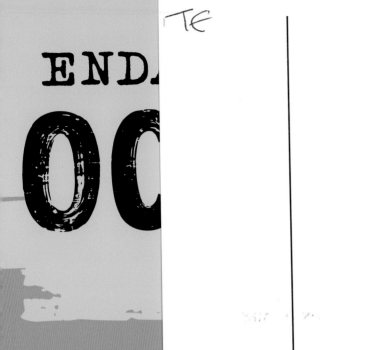

ENDA... ...LIFE

OC...IFE

TE

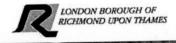

CONTENTS

First published in paperback in Great Britain in 2021 by Wayland

Copyright © Hodder and Stoughton, 2020

Editor: Hayley Fairhead
Design: Elaine Wilkinson

Wayland, an imprint of Hachette Children's Group
Part of Hodder & Stoughton
Carmelite House
50 Victoria Embankment
London EC4Y 0DZ

ISBN: 978 1 5263 0999 0

Printed in Dubai

An Hachette UK Company
www.hachette.co.uk
www.hachettechildrens.co.uk

FSC
MIX
Paper from responsible sources
FSC® C104740
www.fsc.org

Picture acknowledgements: **Alamy:** Bill Bachman 23; Steve Bentley 19t; Mark Conlin 3c,21t, 30tc; anthony grote front cover, 2c, 12-13, 30cl; Images & Stories 19c. **FLPA/Minden Picture**s: Richard Herrmann 7t; Sebastian Kennerknecht 25c; Flip Nicklin 6b; Pete Oxford 29b; Norbert Wu 17. T.A.Jefferson/VIVA Vaquita: 6c, 30cr. **Nature PL:** Matthias Breitner/Minden Pictures 25t; Mark Carwardine 10bl; Suzi Eszterhas/Minden Pictures 24, 30crc; Chris & Monique Fallows 4bl; David Fleetham 8, 30bcl; Jurgen Fruend 9b, 13tr; Remi Masson 26, 30br;Alex Mustard 2t, 4-5, 10-11c, 16, 30tl, 30tcr; Doug Perrine 3t;12cl, 18, 30clc; Todd Pusser 1, 3b, 28, 30bcr;Roland Seitre 14, 15t, 30bl; Nick Upton 27t, 27b; Tony Wu 11b. **REX/Shutterstock:** Auscape/UIG 22, 30tcl;Nic Bothma / EPA-EFE 20. **Shutterstock:** barmalini 9t.
Every attempt has been made to clear copyright. Should there be anyinadvertent omission, please apply to the publisher for rectification.

OCEAN LIFE IN DANGER

Extinction is when a plant or animal dies out. Scientists think that more than 99 per cent of all the species that have ever lived on Earth are extinct. In the past this was due to massive natural events, such as asteroid strikes. Today, thousands of ocean animals face extinction and it's largely down to humans that their future is so uncertain.

OCEAN LIFE

A huge variety of animals live in or on seas and oceans:
- Thousands of species of fish
- Mammals, such as whales
- Reptiles, such as crocodiles
- Birds, such as gulls and terns.

A blue shark preys on a shoal of fish as part of a complex food chain.

Upsetting the balance

Planet Earth is home to an amazing variety of animals and plants. This variety is known as biodiversity, and it is the result of millions of years of evolution. If animals or plants become extinct, there is a loss of biodiversity. In the natural world, the species in a habitat are linked together and rely on each other for their survival. For example, sharks eat smaller fish which, in turn, feed on other fish or sea animals. The loss of even one species in this chain can have a disastrous knock-on effect.

The ocean animals in this book have been given a status rating, set by the IUCN (International Union for the Conservation of Nature). This rating is based on how close to extinction an animal is thought to be. Most of the animals in this book are critically endangered, endangered or vulnerable. Critically endangered means that they face an extremely high risk of becoming extinct in the wild. Endangered means that they are very likely to become extinct in the wild. Vulnerable means that they will probably become endangered unless the threats facing them can be reduced.

Under threat

This book looks at some of the most endangered sea animals. They have been chosen to show the different threats that they face – from habitat loss or overfishing, to collisions with boats or theft of their eggs. The good news is that many governments and conservationists are working hard to save these creatures before it is too late.

A manta ray swims over a coral reef. Many of these rays die when they become entangled in fishing lines.

VAQUITA

A small, dark grey porpoise, the vaquita has a white underside, with dark rings around its mouth and eyes. It swims on its own, or in small groups, feeding mainly on fish, squid and crustaceans.

Vanishing vaquita

The vaquita is found only in the Gulf of California, Mexico, where it lives in warm, shallow lagoons along the shore. Sadly, this rare and beautiful creature is the most endangered sea mammal in the world. In 2007, it was estimated that there were only around 150 vaquita left in the wild, putting it at serious risk of dying out. Since then, numbers have fallen further and, today, there may be only around 30 vaquita left.

A vaquita calf comes to the surface to breathe.

This vaquita has been accidentally caught in a fishing net.

Fatal fishing

The most serious threat facing the vaquita comes from fishing in the Gulf of California. The vaquita get accidentally caught up in fishing nets. They cannot reach the surface to breathe and so they drown. The fish that most fishermen are trying to catch is the totoaba. Like the vaquita, the totoaba is only found in the Gulf and is also critically endangered. It can be sold for large amounts of money in Asia.

Vaquita rescue

Time is running out for the vaquita. Unless urgent action is taken, experts estimate that it could become extinct by 2025, if not before. In 2005, the Mexican Government set up the Vaquita Refuge in the Gulf, where the vaquita are protected and totoaba fishing is banned. Unfortunately, the fishing continues illegally, because the totoaba are so valuable. Conservationists and governments are working to bring about a ban on the trade in totoaba and find alternative ways for the fishermen to earn a living.

Totoaba are valuable fish so fishermen are willing to break the law to catch them.

VITAL STATS

Scientific name:
Phocoena sinus

Length: 120–150 cm

Diet: Fish, squid, crustaceans

Numbers in the wild:
Around 30

Status: Critically endangered

Location: Pacific Ocean
(range marked in red below)

Wild fact

A vaquita can be hard to spot because when it surfaces to breathe, it does so very slowly, hardly making a splash. Then it disappears again.

COMMERCIAL TOP SHELL

The commercial top shell is a species of sea snail – a type of mollusc. It is found in the Indian and Pacific oceans, where it lives on rocks among coral reefs. It grazes on algae and other small plants.

Shell life

The commercial top shell has a large shell, measuring up to 150 mm across its base. The shell is cone-shaped, with cream and reddish-brown stripes. The snail inside has a large, pale brown body, with a pair of long tentacles on its head. At spawning time, females release more than a million eggs which are fertilised by the males. The eggs hatch into tiny larvae that drift on the ocean currents for two years before settling on rocks and turning into adults. Adults can live for up to 15 years.

A commercial top shell can be seen here releasing its tiny green eggs.

Wild fact Empty top shells have been found piled up on coral reefs. It seems that octopuses take them to a particular dining area to snack on!

Mother of pearl

Once widespread in the Indian and Pacific oceans, the commercial top shell has almost disappeared from the waters around several Pacific islands and is becoming rarer on many others. It is harvested for its meat and for its shell. A thick layer of nacre lines the insides of the shell, which can be used to make mother-of-pearl buttons, beads and pendants. Millions of kilogrammes of these shells are collected and exported each year, bringing valuable income to many islanders.

Close-up of a commercial top shell. The inside of the shell is white and pearly.

Commerical top shells are protected by law, but many are still harvested illegally.

VITAL STATS

Scientific name: *Tectus niloticus*

Height: Up to 165 mm

Diet: Algae

Numbers in the wild: Unknown

Status: Not currently classified

Location: Indian Ocean, Pacific Ocean

Shell survival

Today, overfishing is putting the commercial top shell at serious risk. So many shells have been taken that populations do not have time to recover. In addition, the coral reefs where they live are being destroyed by pollution, tourism and tropical storms. Many countries across the topshell's range now reduce fishing for long periods of time to allow new shells to grow. Another priority is to turn the shells' reef habitats into protected marine reserves. There are also plans to release thousands of farmed shells into the wild to increase numbers.

BLUE WHALE

The blue whale is the biggest animal alive today. It can weigh 120,000 kg and grow up to 27 m long. Its heart alone is the size of a small car.

Big eater

Despite its gigantic size, a blue whale mostly eats small, shrimp-like crustaceans, called krill. It has an enormous appetite, however. In summer, when the krill form huge swarms, a whale may eat as much as 4,000 kg every day. Instead of teeth, it has bristly plates, called baleen, hanging down inside its mouth, which it uses to sieve the krill from the water.

A blue whale calf stays with its mother for the first year of its life.

Whale hunting

Until the beginning of the twentieth century, the blue whale was found in every ocean, apart from the Arctic Ocean. But modern whaling equipment spelled disaster for the whales, which were hunted for their meat, oil and bones. Hunting blue whales was banned in 1966, but the blue whale is still threatened by collisions with boats, ocean pollution and getting tangled in fishing nets. Recently, numbers are thought to be increasing but recovery is very slow. Before whaling there were around 300,000 whales in the Southern Ocean. Today, there are between 10,000–25,000 worldwide.

Wild fact

Blue whales have the deepest voices of any animal. Their 'songs' can carry for thousands of kilometres underwater, allowing them to communicate across the vast oceans.

VITAL STATS

Scientific name:
Balaenoptera musculus

Length: Around 25–27 m

Diet: Krill

Numbers in the wild:
10,000–25,000

Status: Endangered

Location: All oceans, except Arctic Ocean

A blue whale dives next to a whale-watching boat. Blue whales can hold their breath underwater for over 20 minutes.

Feeling blue

Working alongside the International Whaling Commission, conservationists and governments have established Marine Protected Areas as sanctuaries for blue whales. In the eastern Pacific Ocean, the WWF (World Wide Fund for Nature) has begun a project to fit satellite tags to a group of blue whales. This will allow them to track the whales and find out vital information about their movements and feeding patterns.

LEATHERBACK TURTLE

The world's largest turtle, the leatherback can measure more than 1.8 m long and weigh almost 1,000 kg. It uses its long front flippers like paddles for propelling itself through the water.

Leatherback turtle hatchlings crawl towards the sea.

Beach birth

Although the leatherback spends most of its time at sea where it feeds on squid and jellyfish, females come ashore to breed. They use their back flippers to dig holes in the sand and lay around 100 eggs inside. After about 60 days, the eggs hatch and the baby turtles dig their way out. They begin their short, but dangerous, journey to the sea, during which many are eaten by seabirds and crabs.

Turtle trouble

Over the last 20 years, leatherback turtle numbers have fallen fast. Thousands of turtles are accidentally caught in fishing nets and drown because they cannot reach the surface to breathe. Thousands more are killed by eating plastic bags dumped in the sea, which the turtles mistake for jellyfish. Many vital nesting beaches are being destroyed by the building of tourist resorts, while tens of thousands of turtle eggs are illegally collected for food. In Malaysia, this has already led to the leatherback becoming extinct.

Beach rescue

Conservation groups, such as the WWF and the Leatherback Trust, are working to safeguard the turtles' nesting beaches. In some places, beaches have been set aside as sanctuaries, patrolled by teams of local rangers. This has seen good results on beaches in Costa Rica, where up to 100 per cent of turtle eggs used to be poached.

Turtle eggs in Indonesia are relocated to a safer nesting place.

Leatherback turtles swim long distances to reach their breeding sites.

VITAL STATS

Scientific name:
Dermochelys coriacea

Length: Up to 1.8 m

Diet: Mostly jellyfish, squid

Numbers in the wild:
Around 2,300 (Pacific Ocean);
30,000 (Atlantic Ocean)

Status: Vulnerable

Location: Pacific Ocean,
Atlantic Ocean

Wild fact The leatherback turtle can dive down to depths of over 1,000 m – deeper than any other turtle – in search of jellyfish to eat. It can hold its breath for up to 85 minutes.

SOUTHERN BLUEFIN TUNA

With its powerful, streamlined body, the southern bluefin tuna is one of the fastest fish in the sea. While the tuna usually cruises through the ocean at around 2-3 km per hour, it is capable of reaching a staggering top speed of 70 km per hour!

Tuna travels

Southern bluefin tuna are among the biggest bony fish, growing up to 2.5 m long and weighing up to 200 kg. They swim in large shoals, travelling vast distances from their breeding grounds in the Indian Ocean around Indonesia to their feeding grounds around south-western Australia, where they eat smaller fish and squid.

Southern bluefin tuna gather in enormous shoals.

Taste for tuna

Southern bluefin tuna are highly prized as food, especially in Japan. Thousands of kilogrammes of tuna are caught every year, and a single fish can sell for thousands of pounds. Modern fishing fleets are equipped with high-tech satellites, GPS and radar which allow them to locate tuna shoals easily. Today, overfishing has pushed the southern bluefin tuna to the edge of extinction. Since the 1980s, its numbers have fallen by more than 90 per cent.

Southern bluefin tuna are raised and fished on this farm in south Australia to reduce the numbers of wild tuna fished from the oceans.

Fishing limits

Since the 1990s, many of the countries that fish for tuna have signed up to the Commission for the Conservation of the southern bluefin tuna. This organisation aims to protect the tuna, largely by placing strict limits on the numbers of tuna allowed to be caught. This should give the tuna time to recover, though many conservationists think that too little is being done, too late.

VITAL STATS

Scientific name:
Thunnus maccoyii

Length: Up to 2.5 m

Diet: Fish, squid, crustaceans

Numbers in the wild: Unknown

Status: Critically endangered

Location: Oceans in the Southern Hemisphere

Wild fact Southern bluefin tuna can survive in cold water because their blood is specially adapted to hold heat, keeping their bodies warmer than the water around them.

GREAT HAMMERHEAD SHARK

Reaching up to 6 m, this enormous shark is famous for its huge hammer-shaped head. Its eyes are located at either end of the hammer, with its mouth underneath. This unusual arrangement allows the shark to scan the ocean floor for food.

A great hammerhead shark swims off the Bahamas in the Atlantic Ocean.

Stingray supper

Great hammerhead sharks are found along the coasts of warm seas around the world. They feed mainly on stingrays. The shark pins a stingray down on the sea floor with its hammer, then bites chunks from the ray's wings with its serrated, triangular teeth. Incredibly, most sharks aren't harmed by the stingray's poisonous tail spines, which are often found sticking inside their mouths.

Wild fact

A great hammerhead hunts at dusk, swinging its head from side to side over the sea floor to pick up electrical signals from stingrays buried in the sand.

Shark fin soup

The main threat facing the great hammerhead is fishing. Its large, pointed back fin is used in Asia for making shark fin soup. Once the fin has been cut off, the rest of the shark is thrown back into the water, often alive. Without its fin, it cannot swim, and dies. Hammerhead sharks are also often accidentally caught in fishing nets because of the unique shape of their head.

Save a shark

A great hammerhead shark can live for 20–30 years, but because it only breeds every two years, its numbers are declining. Some countries, including Australia and the USA, are now banning the removal of shark fins. Unfortunately, this practice continues illegally. In some places, such as the Bahamas, diving with hammerheads has become popular with tourists. Properly managed, it is hoped that this will help to raise awareness of the sharks and the need to protect them.

VITAL STATS

Scientific name:
Sphyrna mokarran
Length: Up to 6 m
Diet: Stingrays, fish
Numbers in the wild: Unknown
Status: Critically endangered
Location: Worldwide

A diver meets a great hammerhead shark.

MEDITERRANEAN MONK SEAL

One of the world's most endangered mammals, the Mediterranean monk seal was once widespread around the Mediterranean and Black seas. Today, it only lives in a few, small colonies off Greece, Turkey and northern Africa.

Nursery caves

The Mediterranean monk seal lives in warm water around the coast, where it spends the day foraging for fish, squid and octopus. At breeding time, females come out of the sea to breed on sandy beaches or in rocky caves. They give birth to a single pup. Mother and pup have a strong bond and stay together for up to three years.

A Mediterranean monk seal swims in the sea near Portugal.

Struggling seals

In ancient times, seeing a monk seal was thought to be lucky. Over the centuries, so many have been hunted for their skin, meat and oil that they have almost disappeared. In the last 50 years alone, scientists estimate seal numbers have fallen by around 60 per cent. The seals are still hunted and killed by fishermen who see them as competition for their catch. Pollution threatens their habitat in the busy Mediterranean Sea and the coastlines along which they rest and breed are being developed for tourism.

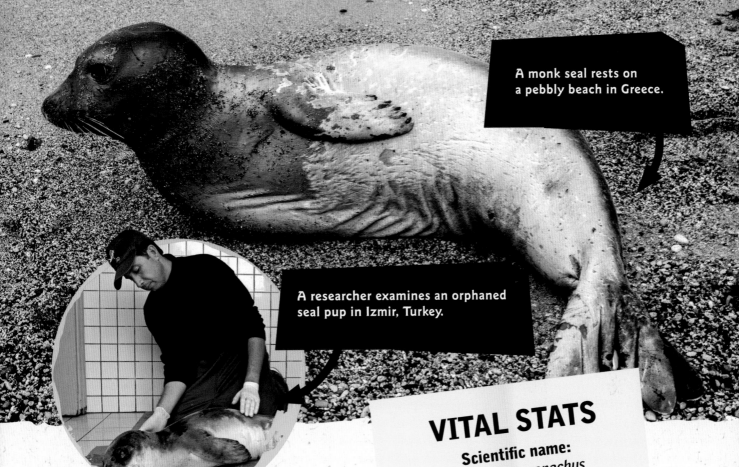

A monk seal rests on a pebbly beach in Greece.

A researcher examines an orphaned seal pup in Izmir, Turkey.

Action plan

The Mediterranean monk seal is protected by law across its range, but urgent action is needed to save it. To protect the seals' breeding caves, monitored reserves have been set up. Observers are also being placed on boats to prevent the seals getting tangled up in fishing gear. These measures seem to be working. In some countries where monk seals have been absent for a long time, such as Croatia, they have been spotted again.

VITAL STATS

Scientific name: *Monachus monachus*

Length: Up to 2.8 m

Diet: Fish, squid, octopus

Numbers in the wild: 250–350

Status: Endangered

Location: Atlantic Ocean

Wild fact Monk seals got their name because their smooth, brownish-grey coats were thought to look like a monk's robes.

KNYSNA SEAHORSE

The delicate Knysna (Cape) seahorse lives among thickets of sea grass up to 20 m below the surface of the water. Here, it is perfectly camouflaged by its mottled black and brown colouring. It grasps seagrass stalks with its tail to stop the current carrying it away.

Caring father

Seahorses are unusual fish because it is the male who carries the eggs until they hatch. During breeding, the female transfers her eggs to a pouch on the male's front. There, they grow and develop for 2–3 weeks until they hatch. Then the young swim out of the pouch and their father leaves them to look after themselves.

Shrinking range

Hundreds of thousands of Knysna seahorses once lived along the south coast of South Africa. Sadly, their numbers have fallen by half in the last ten years and, today, they are only found in the estuaries of three rivers. Some are poached for the pet trade or to be used in alternative medicines, but the fall in their numbers is mainly due to the loss of their habitat, as more people move to live along the coast. Waste water and sewage pollute the water and boats damage the sea grass beds.

The Knysna seahorse is caught and used for alternative medicines. It is thought to help treat asthma and some skin problems.

Knysna seashorses are cared for in Two Oceans Aquarium in South Africa.

VITAL STATS

Scientific name:
Hippocampus capensis

Length: Around 10 cm

Diet: Small crustaceans

Numbers in the wild:
Fewer than 100,000

Status: Endangered

Location: Atlantic Ocean

Save the seahorse

The first seahorse to be declared endangered, the Knysna seahorse is now protected by law in South Africa. Several projects, such as the Knysna Seahorse Status Project, have been started to protect the seahorse and get local people involved in saving it. There are captive-breeding programmes at the Two Oceans Aquarium in Cape Town and Belgium's Antwerp Zoo. This captive-bred stock will be used to supply aquaria and the pet trade, to avoid seahorses being poached from the wild.

Wild fact Knysna seahorses feed on small crustaceans living on seagrass stalks. They do not have stomachs and digest their food so quickly that they need to eat almost non-stop.

LARGETOOTH SAWFISH

Belonging to the same group of bony fish as sharks, skates and rays, the largetooth sawfish lives along the coasts of tropical oceans. It can also survive in freshwater rivers and lakes.

Super saw

One of the world's largest fish, the largetooth sawfish can grow up to 7 m long. Its long saw-like mouth makes up to a quarter of its length, and its edges are lined with long, sharp teeth. The sawfish is a predator, feeding on fish, crustaceans and molluscs. It uses its saw to slash at shoals of fish and to dig up sand and mud to find prey. Young sawfish hatch from eggs inside their mother. To protect her, their saws are soft and bendy, and their teeth do not harden until after their birth.

A largetooth sawfish lies on the sea bottom in Australia.

Vanishing fast

The largetooth sawfish was once widespread in warmer parts of the Atlantic and Pacific oceans. Today, it is extinct or very rare across much of its range. It is hunted for its fins, which are made into shark fin soup, and for its saws, which are sold as ornaments. Their saw is also easily entangled in fishing nets. In Australia, fishermen should by law release the sawfish alive, but these large fish can be difficult to handle and often die anyway.

Save a sawfish

Without urgent action, it seems unlikely that the largetooth sawfish will survive. In 2012, conservationists from around the world met in London to address the sawfishes' plight. International trade in sawfish body parts is now banned and work is being done to find out more about the fish, especially how they breed. In some places, such as Australia, the sawfish are protected, but this is not yet the case everywhere.

VITAL STATS

Scientific name: *Pristis pristis*

Length: up to 7 m

Diet: Small fish, crustaceans

Numbers in the wild: Unknown

Status: Critically endangered

Location: Atlantic Ocean, Pacific Ocean

Conservationists examine a largetooth sawfish.

Wild fact The 'teeth' on a sawfish's saw are not actually teeth but a type of scale. The sawfish's real teeth are inside its mouth, on its underside.

SEA OTTER

Sea otters are well adapted for life in the sea. Their large back feet work like flippers, and they steer with their rudder-like tails. Their thick fur coats keep them warm and dry.

Upside-down otter

A sea otter dives to the sea bed to find sea urchins, mussels and crabs to eat. It carries them to the surface in pouches of skin under its armpits. Then it lies on its back and uses its chest as a table to open the shells, sometimes smashing them with a rock. Pups are also carried on the female's chest, while she nurses them and grooms their fur.

A sea otter cares for her pup off the coast of California, USA.

Wild fact California sea otters sleep on their backs in the water. They wind strands of seaweed around their bodies to stop themselves drifting away on ocean currents.

Fatal fur trade

Once found in large numbers along the North Pacific coasts of Russia and the USA, sea otters were hunted almost to extinction for their highly prized fur. By 1900, there were fewer than 2,000 left, down from hundreds of thousands a century earlier. Worst hit were the Californian otters whose numbers fell as low as 50. Today, sea otter numbers have risen again, but they are still extremely rare, and are threatened by ocean pollution, oil spills and entanglement in fishing gear.

Sea otters float in the waters off Alaska.

A rescued sea otter pup in Monterey Bay Aquarium in California is wrapped in fake kelp to prepare it for being released back into the wild.

Sea otter rescue

Sea otters are now protected, and many conservation organisations are working on their behalf. At the Monterey Bay Aquarium in California, stranded or injured otters are rescued and nursed back to health. Radio transmitters are fitted to track them once they are released back into the wild. This information helps scientists to understand the threats to the sea otters and work towards the species' recovery.

VITAL STATS

Scientific name:
Enhydra lutris
Length: Around 150 cm
Diet: Sea urchins, mussels, crabs
Numbers in the wild:
Around 125,000
Status: Endangered
Location: Pacific Ocean

EUROPEAN EEL

A long, snake-like fish, the European eel can grow up to 1.5 m long. It is unusual because it spends part of its life in freshwater and part in the sea.

An adult European eel swims down the River Rhône in France.

Eel travellers

A European eel spawns in the Sargasso Sea, in the North Atlantic Ocean. The eggs hatch into larvae which look like curled leaves. For the next three years, the larvae drift on the ocean currents towards coasts of Europe. After the larvae hatch, the young eels swim up rivers and spend up to 20 years growing into adults. As adults, they travel thousands of kilometres back to the sea to lay their eggs. They can live for up to 85 years.

Wild fact Eels change colour as they mature. Elvers (young eels) are so transparent that you could read a newspaper through them! Adult eels are black, brown or dark green.

Edible eels

Eels used to be common in Europe but their numbers have fallen by up to 95 per cent in the last 25 years. In some places, they have disappeared completely. The main threat comes from overfishing – eels are a very popular food in Asia and Europe. Dams and weirs are also increasingly blocking the eels' migration routes, and stopping the young eels being able to swim up the rivers where they mature. This problem may well get worse as more hydro-electric schemes are built along rivers.

Young eels are released into a lake in Wales.

VITAL STATS

Scientific name:
Anguilla anguilla

Length: Up to 1.5 m

Diet: Molluscs, crustaceans, fish

Numbers in the wild: Unknown

Status: Critically endangered

Location: Atlantic Ocean and European rivers

Eel lifeline

Already critically endangered, urgent action is needed to save the European eel from extinction. An international recovery plan has been launched and strict limits put on eel fishing. In England and Wales, the Environment Agency has built 'eel ladders' on some rivers. These are ramps and steps that help the eels to swim past obstacles, such as dams. On other rivers, young eels are trapped, then released further upstream once they are clear of barriers. The eels are also tagged to help scientists understand their movements better.

A young eel wriggles up an eel ladder as it swims upstream.

WEST INDIAN MANATEE

More closely related to elephants than to whales, a manatee is a large, round sea mammal with a bristly snout. Its front limbs are short and flipper-like and it uses its tail like a paddle.

A West Indian manatee calf will stay with its mother for one to two years.

Manatee lifestyle

The West Indian manatee lives along the coasts of the eastern USA, Gulf of Mexico and Caribbean Sea. It spends hours at a time grazing on sea grass that grows under the water, coming to the surface to breathe every few minutes. Manatees have to venture up rivers and creeks to get freshwater for drinking. They can live for more than 50 years, but only have one calf every two years.

Fatal collisions

In the past, the greatest danger facing the manatee was being hunted for its meat, oil and skin. Today, most manatee deaths are caused by collisions with boats and jet skis. Manatees also get tangled in fishing gear and are suffering from habitat loss.

VITAL STATS

Scientific name:
Trichechus manatus

Length: Up to 4 m

Diet: Sea grass

Numbers in the wild:
More than 6,000

Status: Vulnerable

Location: Atlantic Ocean

Wild fact

When a manatee's molar teeth get old or worn out, new teeth grow up in the back of its jaws and push forward to replace them. This can happen many times in a lifetime.

An orphaned West Indian manatee calf is bottle-fed at the Manatee Rehabilitation Centre in Belize.

Road to recovery

By the 1970s, there were only a few hundred West Indian manatees left in the wild. Thanks to a range of conservation measures, numbers have now increased to more than 6,000. In the USA, manatee protection areas have been set up, with signs warning boat operators to slow down. There are also schemes in place for recycling fishing lines, rather than dumping them in the water. The manatees in the protected areas are carefully monitored and given regular health checks.

LOCATOR MAP

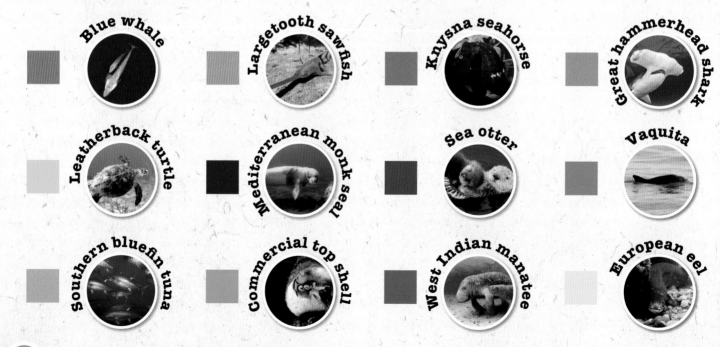

Blue whale

Largetooth sawfish

Knysna seahorse

Great hammerhead shark

Leatherback turtle

Mediterranean monk seal

Sea otter

Vaquita

Southern bluefin tuna

Commercial top shell

West Indian manatee

European eel

GLOSSARY

Algae Tiny plants.

Baleen Rows of bony plates that hang down inside some whales' mouths.

Camouflaged When the natural colouring, patterns or shape of an animal help it to blend in with its surroundings.

Captive breeding When endangered animals are bred in captivity, in zoos or wildlife reserves.

Colony A group of animals that lives together.

Conservationist Scientist or other person who works to protect endangered wildlife and habitats

Crustacean Animal, such as a lobster, shrimp or crab, that has a hard shell and mostly lives in the sea.

Endangered In danger of becoming extinct.

Estuary Where a river flows into the sea, and fresh water mixes with salty water.

Extinct Describing an animal or plant that has died out.

Fertilised When a male adds his sperm to a female's egg so that a baby can grow.

GPS (Global Positioning System) A system that uses satellites to fix locations and draw up accurate maps.

Habitat The natural home of an animal or plant.

Hydro-electric Describing something that makes electricity using flowing water.

Lagoon Shallow pond near or linked to a larger body of water.

Larvae The young of some animals.

Mollusc An animal, such as a snail, sea shell, squid or octopus.

Nacre Another word for mother-of-pearl.

Poached When endangered animals are illegally hunted and caught.

Porpoise A sea mammal related to whales and dolphins.

Predator An animal that hunts and kills other animals for food.

Prey Animals that are hunted by other animals for food.

Seagrass A plant with narrow, grass-like leaves that grows in shallow coastal waters.

Serrated Having a jagged edge.

Shoal Large group of fish.

Spawning (time) The time of year when fish and other animals produce their young.

FURTHER INFORMATION

https://newredlist.iucnredlist.org
The website for the IUCN (International Union for Conservation of Nature) Red List of endangered animals and plants.

www.edgeofexistence.org
A programme set up with the ZSL (Zoological Society of London) to highlight and conserve endangered animals.

www.worldwildlife.org/species
The website of the WWF (World Wide Fund for Nature) with information about endangered animals, and conservation projects.

INDEX